What Island

Poetry Winner
First Book Contest
sponsored by MFA in Creative
Writing Program at Fairleigh
Dickinson University and
Serving House Books

What Island

P. K. Harmon

SERVING HOUSE BOOKS

What Island

Copyright © 2011 P. K. Harmon

All rights reserved.

No part of this book may be used or reproduced in any manner whatsoever without the prior written permission of the copyright holder except for brief quotations in critical articles or reviews.

ISBN: 978-0-9838289-3-8

Cover art by Mark Hackworth

Author photo by Likilimej

Serving House Books logo by Barry Lereng Wilmont

Published by Serving House Books
Copenhagen and Florham Park, NJ

www.servinghousebooks.com

First Serving House Books Edition 2011
Second Serving House Books Edition 2015

Buk in ej nan
　　　　　Meto
　　　　　　im Melu

M.I.F. 210

P. K. Harmon meditates on the limits of the rational mind in its encounters with the mysteries of Nature, Chance, and Time. As he contemplates human efforts to control the energies of life, his responses range from well-informed anger at society's destructiveness to a charming humility about the individual's power to resist the pressures of history. Harmon's poetry vibrates with the tension between dreaminess and responsibility; the theme is crystallized in these lines from the poem "What Foot": "I get way out there on the water in the sky / feeling pretty beautiful actually but then look down / to my foot and the print it inevitably has to make." Here is a poet who finds himself in a Micronesian world that is in some ways paradisal, yet threatened by economic and environmental forces that can't be escaped anywhere. Most of the time Harmon is both amazed and happy in the choices he has made—though doubts can suddenly spring up, as we sense in "What Lagoon 3": "Lagoon brown lagoon blue. / I am not trapped I am not / trapped I am not trapped I am / not trapped I am not." Despite that fear, the keynote in Harmon's vision is an affectionate bemusement which at moments attains to spiritual peacefulnes—peaceful yet not sleepy—alert, humorous, ever-ready to discover hope. Readers who love William Stafford, Gary Snyder or Galway Kinnell will find Harmon's voice charismatic, oddly authoritative, and salubrious.

—Mark Halliday

Table of Contents

One

What Wave / 13
What Birth / 14
What Blue / 15
What May / 16
What Moon / 17
What Love / 18
What Shape / 19
What I Say / 20
What Island / 21
What Lips / 22
What Sleep / 23
What Water & Light / 24
What For / 25
What Letter / 26
What Bob / 27

Two

What Moment / 35
What Possibilities / 36
What Waiting / 38
What Thought / 39
What Song / 40
What Prayer / 41
What Obligation / 42
What the Neighbor's Wife Said / 43
What Foot / 45
What Drama / 47
What Dignity / 49
What the Gecko Said / 50

What City / 51
What Affliction / 53
What Answers / 54
What Drifting / 55
What Leapt / 57

Three

What Identity / 61
What If / 62
What Happened / 63
What Bikini / 65

What Lagoon 1 - 7 / 69

What I Called Desire / 76
What Was What Is / 78
What Fetus / 79
Whatever / 80

One

What Wave

There is a wheel barrow
minus its wheel—that is
for cans. Glass goes in

an old cooler that washed up.
Mornings we rake into little
piles to burn at night
and there is where we cook,
by the big shallow that

fills at high tide. All day
we keep an eye out front
for those little fish that
make good bait for the bigger

kind but mostly we are just
sleeping. Everyday that boy
our child does something new

and maybe nothing of this
life will remain with him
except a vague sort of wave.

What Birth

There is a little grass
hopper a pale neon green
as if it has only just
been borne out of some

spit sack crawling up
from the water catchment
to my place above the lagoon
where I sit tap tapping

on the typewriter to the wind
and the tiny clothes and
blankets that the wind flaps
and snaps like tiny flags

of a nation of easy going
sleepers, the tiny garments
of my infant son. That little
bug is really holding on

and it is most impressive
because there is pretty much
nothing I can do to insure
the safety of its progress.

What Blue

There was no stopping
but when I tired I put on a mask
and fell over—how true it was
like flying. The sandy bottom
a desert blooming a patched

garden and two big turtles
as surprised as myself to be
here, older than sunken volcanoes.
I wish I could say how blue

and how we turned from one
another into blue—all so blue
those old beaks cutting ahead
the flapping somehow grace too

in the flight—those two into
a deeper and deeper blue and I
drifted closer and closer
to the rough and sharp until

finally the heavy air that is
coming into a lovely silence.

What May

They were pipers and not terns
and there they huddled is the word
(not "sitting" as I had said)
against the wing a strong wind.

I can see them now down on the sea
wall and if the weather remains
so we will too. Somewhere up
in the lofted ceiling a gecko is

laughing. We sprawl around all
day like a pack of animals. The boy
has a woven mat he plays on, crawls
on, sleeps on and it gets moved

around the house throughout the day—
a mat of woven pandanus, a magic pandanus
carpet, its weave a source of serious
contemplation for his newly found

hands. Today is a revision. Today
is a storm and its aftermath. Today
our shirts collect wind like sails,
like wings. Any moment we'll be tossed.

What Moon

The moon is a turtle on its back.
Do you ever feel like that? Or,

the moon is a boat skimming the water
it illuminates and maybe you better

get on board. I stood and the rain
gently began to fall. Then it really

fell for serious and the moon sank.
Or it turned over and swam away.

Either way, the moon is gone. And
memory, once on its back, well

it's tough getting up after that.

What Love

In the morning, in an afternoon
that felt like a morning: the angel
skin of the mosquito net; her combed
and oiled black hair blurred against

the pale green undersides of the nin
tree leaves out the window; the child's

experiments with voice, sound; my vague
loneliness and sudden arousals under
the crackling tin roof's expansion
in the sun and heat. All of it

was something that could have happened.
Maybe happening now and with baby's
laughter. Three terns not hunting sit
on the sea wall and face the wind.

So what. I guess this is not doing
something. My love poem is bored
but in love. I call for more wind.

When it arrives nothing has changed.
True story: we lived on a tiny island
when you were a tiny boy full of laughter
and when I got nothing right you were.

What Shape

Why do clouds puff and stack?
Miles high some of them, in a circle
around an atoll, which is a circle
too, sort of. They do, pretty often.

The water, just now the color you'd expect
it to be but a little while before was

an impossible shade of green, boils
with a school of something
in front of us while black noddies
and their bleached white heads white

as clouds circle sort of in a frenzy
over top the spot. That is the lagoon.

Back there, the ocean. The tide nearly
high so the two are really the same
so the next island over, that little
perfect circle of itself, is like a submerged

head in need. I don't know what all this
waiting is for but I am.

What I Say

Twice an angel tern
stood in the air
above my head.
Twenty-some baby sharks

came to my shore.
What was it that I was
afraid of back in that
other life? I stand

on reef so smooth
my feet darken to it
and somewhere on the small
island my son is learning
to crawl. I finally don't
care there is nothing fancy
in what I say.

What Island

In the tiniest of tide pools
is reflected the faintest
of stars in a night with no more
moon. I am thinking of words

something along these lines
in the dark, caught by this
little glint, little real image,
when the darkest girl, the mother

of our child, says "The ocean is
eating the island we stand on."
After a pause punctuated by the ocean
eating the island, she asks "Are the words

I say broken?" And because we are
shadows in the Earth's shadow
and it is enough to just think
I say *not at all.*

What Lips

In the morning
   I drifted away
on a boat—

at noon I watched
   her dark lips
purse like a net.

By the afternoon
   I was myself
a carrier of dreams.

This evening
   I will place a flame
near the lapping

so that in the night
   I may glimpse
some final thought.

In the morning
   I may drift
away so.

What Sleep

How am I to know the taste of sky?
By observing the shape of one of her clouds?

It is a coconut, slowly falling.
It is something else entirely.

A hint of green. What is it?
Once I think I must have known.

I remain very much asleep.
I have struggled to recall the language required

and I remain very much asleep. More clouds
arrive: an aggregation. Things shaping up. But still

how am I to know the taste of sky?
Can she see herself reflected

in the lagoon? What scrap of language am I
neglecting that would help? I remain asleep.

There is a sense that the sky waits patiently,
she is almost bored, oh she is beautifully bored.

What Water & Light

Dawn hits the lagoon

It is not unusual to see
rainbows at this hour, over
the lagoon

But water does strange things:

Like what's this? Not
a colorful arching of color
(rainbow) as expected
but a shaft, a straight line
that just extends ever up

not arching
no curvature of earth

just up as if
the earth were itself
a stick

and not a ball

Dawn will not last
by definition

And no one else will

believe me

What For

My listening ears are filled with water—
my own walking on sand and crushed
coral is a sound inside
and I am walking away from myself to
what cannot be heard. And

my sleeping body left in shadow stays
in shadow as light is moved in lines
around it—my own dreaming whole,
certain, a body of water—
irretrievable as a passing wave
passing with other waves. So

my speaking voice is empty—
its tone faint fronds on the air.
My seeing eyes look into the blue space;
my tasting tongue has only clean
bones like tide-smooth shells and
my feeling hands have only

the water of a sleeper's dream, of
faint air, of blue space, and of the tongue
and also the water in the listening ears
which when heard sounds exactly like
nothing but itself …

What Letter

In a letter I don't write I tell her
about the path to and from

the beach all shaded and cave-like
a series of hands cupping, a tunnel

of foliage the great breadfruit trees some
big mighty big twisting trunks and limbs

weaving in and out of one another
and Dr. Seuss inspired pandanus spilling up
under these fireworks frozen green
neon-green after rain lush lush

when tide is out the wide flat line
angel terns argue over torment their own
thieving and screaming and oh further

out there noddies pushing themselves
from the air to plunge into the salty
spray of their own diving their own doing

What Bob

    1
By the corner of the house
  is the fire where I cook
and because the house is new
  to me, the island new
too, maybe beautiful maybe
  because of these things
I look around not exactly
  uneasily but curiously
and the first night at the house
  the new house on the new
island I think I see someone
  standing at the corner
of the house by the fire
  I turn and every time
get a little start thinking
  I see this figure which
it turns out is a tree.

    2
The little tree by the fire
  at the corner of the house
seems a figure still in the
  light of the next day
even in the primary noon the blue
  brightness of the island
so I say ok you are a figure
  I say hello Bob I'll call
you Bob. Is Bob some kind of ghost?
  Last night I woke thinking
the wind but it was just
  Bob closing the door. Now

I think I'm pretty sure I know
   this Bob from somewhere
before but how? This is a new
   island to me. I hear slapping
waves: Bob is swimming.

      3

Is that rain? No. Is it leaves
   falling? Not that either. I had
put just right in my mind earlier
   today that the sun was heating
up the tin—Is that it? Nope.
   It's Bob! He's dancing on the
roof this morning he was dancing
   up there. You must be a happy
thing, Bob. What you mean, he says.
   I stop right there because it's
nuts talking this way. You gave me
   this name didn't you? I'm thinking
he wrote the book I'm reading. I'm sure
   he put the book together. Or I could
have dreamt it because this
   new island is a sleepy island.
Because it is I'm not telling
   anyone. Not even me, says Bob.

      4

I have regrets about Bob.
   I am heavy and sleepy.
I've collected some wood
   and looked to the small
tree. What is making
   the fever on my brow?
Because I didn't like the last
   dream I had I went to

sleep again. Bob was there.
   I go put a stick on the dying
embers and look at the little
    tree. Hello.

       5
Put another chair, set a place
   for Bob. Though he has a
common name he brings me good
    cheer: We
it turns out have much in
   common. We've said very little
all day comfortably idle in
   the house. Bob is
and is not a little tree. What's
   he doing in the loft? What's he
doing on the roof now? Didn't
   I just see you on the other
side of this little island?
   Yes, you did. Last night I
frightened up some birds there.

       6
Did you? said Bob.
   I think you need
to drink more water.
   Mind if I sing along?
If you know the words.
   I'll hum if I don't.
Now's a good time.
   For what, Bob?
Put your hand out.
   What's in it when
the mind takes hold.
   Didn't Bob say that?

Maybe I've known him
   all along. So this is
where you live. No, it
   isn't. Are you sleepy
yet again? Bob? What.

      7
I'm going in the water.
   Ok. Well, not just yet.
You've left your shoes on
   the reef. I only have one.
I see that. Bob has a ukulele
   but uses the strings for
something I don't know what.
   I'm going to burn the little
thing because he wants me
   to I guess. The fact that
most know him by Robert gives
   me some measure of pride.
It's only been one day after
   all. He's as inept at spelling
as I am: just look at the
   arrangement of broken coral
on the shore. Is that one
   shoe there? Yep.

      8
Something
   is floating I bet. Something
is snagged but not forever. And
   at the corner something stands.
The primary sky over the primary
   water is as clear as I want
it to be. Sleep is a thing that
   is punctuated. I do not hope

but nevertheless I will
   read from Bob's book if it is
Bob's book. It is, says Bob.

Two

What Moment

and now and now and now
(but you'll be wanting some explanation;
but really it's feedback you want,
reflection of your *self*, that's it isn't it;
to reflect on you and you and you
but you don't like it and something
in you stiffens—how boring
with all this stuff of the island that you
stand on! We agreed to give pause
once a week a week a week—
sit here awhile; look there at the sun
dipping down, the end-of-the-world
seiners lighting up, the blackening
lagoon, the awakening rats in the wall,
the pretty clouds stacking up miles,
the mercury bulbs flickering on around,
the slight shift of wind and the meria tree
pushing out its white stars, the words
you own rumbling about not quite what

you meant them to say—
you meant them to say—
you meant them to say

look at me, I'm right here with
you and that's the sound of water
because I just now tossed it there).

What Possibilities

My friend Gary has a new job a good one
so I say oh good now maybe I can borrow money
off of you now and we laugh at this and then talk
turns to others things—recent crimes on this end of the island
an upcoming sports event on the tube his boy's
obsession with PlayStation—but like my very reliable
yet very scary-to-look-at car Gary says do you have
any money I can borrow until Wednesday? and I
say No and for two reasons and I say this so certainly
that I sort of surprise myself…one, I don't have
any right now. What's two? he wonders and I admit
there is no two. We look at the breadfruit leaves
rustle around or whatever in the breeze and we are
leaning on his new blue pick-up there in the shade
by the laundry. Well says Gary see you. Okay I say.
                                                              Over

at the house the sun is really cooking and it isn't
yet noon and some fish are jumping out clear out
of the water which is all silvery but the fish are
even more silvery and I can see that someone has
tied up some kind of large plastic part to a jungle
gym to my buoy and I think okay that's okay that's
pretty neat actually I mean with the possibilities
of this new piece of junk around so I think of some
and they all seem pretty good pretty doable and
the day just goes on like this and pretty soon it is
a whole bunch of days maybe even a couple
three year's worth with okay not large plastic jungle
gym parts every time showing up to my little
part of the lagoon but a whole parade of strange
stuff strangeness on parade punctuated with you

strange people who are it turns out my friends
come to check out the silvery fish leap out of
the silvery water with me and spread your strange
strange lives out for my what-turns-out-to-be
gentle gaze, and to think of a use for us all.

What Waiting

I'm trying out the engagement ring
someone on the TV says *you look lost*
and that's where my outer island
family gathers amazed

or I am spinning the ring
lefty-like in the other room
I am outside playing folk on the island
strings just before it rains

I can never be alone again
she watches me write
and the remaining year is this
delicious question mark

excepting the child
expecting the child
accepting our child

something is curling at my mouth
she moans in ways I cannot explain

I thought I was through trying
to get it down but I'm not

So it's clear, here: I was already a father
I have always been on island
(Not enough?) here: wahoo banana cold can of beer
rice coconut breadfruit one more sure skip jack

What Thought

I don't ever want to be any colder than
jumping in the lagoon at seven in the morning

and I sort of announce this with
the brave truth morning allows for

to Jimmy as he rouses from an anxious sort of dream
about a game of cricket had on my little day bed

there in the living room. Bright sunlight and rain and then
a rainbow. This is rainbow season

Jimmy says and I realize again, because *remember*
doesn't quite express it, I realize again how important

is a little carelessness to getting a day to happen.
One of us has written a poem about a papaya—

one of us has left a papaya at the door
and I do eat the fruit—I drink a little

beer too and happily go to work

What Song

There was a moment, very late into the party
in the yard between the door and the lagoon

when the host reached a sort of drunken
epiphany of performance by singing a song

about (while simultaneously drinking) tequila
then puking into his beer, still playing, even

adding a little verse about puking. He possessed
a certain lucid state despite or because of

the drunkenness. Glorious! Then the next day
he experienced a real physical train wreck

which put him in the hospital on valium and oxygen
during which he puked, a little more

painfully this time, and very much alone.
But the song! Glorious!

What Prayer

Ragged fading nail polish on
Sunday and some Champaign.
There is Nellie and her poems,
Her turning them on the stove.

Today, now, I am my ragged self:
Faded, given to whatever indulgence.
This page, that page.
O little lovely time ago!

This is waiting.
This is the ocean boiling as if.

Just play a tune, stupid.
Just go on with yourself.
(What sort of prayer is this?)
Plug it in and turn it up.

What is playing now
In the movie
Of my mind,
You big God of Doubt?

What Obligation

Grandmother is picking leaves
       off the flowering bush
flowering red no blood lavender
       she shall pick until bare branched
and the leaves come back
       and the flowers flower
and the grandmother

She has beaten a path around the house

She is remembering and then forgetting

She knocks upon her own door

What the Neighbor's Wife Said

There is no synonym for betrothal
There is only my hair up
This child of mine sick my uncertain
Tongue on the edges of
This white language

I can almost hear the world
Before air conditioning

I am promised to him I do not know
My child has no father for now I will
Only speak of it in this way

I can almost remember
How to smell what
The rain in the specked horizon means

I do not speak in this way
No other words can be substituted
For the way my hair is up
This dress fitting the way it does
This child of mine
I do not even know somehow

I cannot remember how I arrived
To this age but I am yes I am
Willing to open his cans to walk
Lightly around just this side
Of his ways I think I know them
After all there is a TV to help me
Almost recognize a world

This is what I know of what he wants
My hair is pulled back and up
I still the child my child I pretend
This white language I hear coming
Out of my mouth this is how I would
Speak how I would behave so to speak
Between advertisements I've seen it so

I imagine the wind and shark skin
Stretched and patted for my dead
Mother's mother's mother's mother
Before the songs must have started I imagine
To just float away on the breezes just sweep

Across this island that seems to be shrinking
Would be to almost recollect a world that is
Leaving I can do this because I am saying
I want this I can do this but why he does not
Know what to say I will not say I will only say
This is not how we ever spoke

What Foot

My foot is the obvious thing (to me
as I'm thinking of it now), a metaphor
for stepping on keys that unfold letters
that unfold words, words that had been unfolded
before and are the same as those unfolding
now and, well, would be as much the same
obfuscated ripple of syllables as they ever
were, were they the words they were
but they are not it turns out.
                        The thing is I haven't done this
in a what-feels-like long while and the foot
print, the *font*, is the very one I remember
using to hammer out that shitty manuscript—
is it ten years ago?—of simply heartfelt chaos,
Confusion first-mate of every boat that I sailed
and eventually learned how not to turn over.
A heavy foot, you see. It becomes reckless word
after reckless word and then line and then
stanza, utterance and breath, sound
then silence. So I am reminded by the look
of the letters, the shape of the space they reside
in and the sort of handsome droopiness they
mostly pull off, reminded of a time of productivity
with words, an output that was brave I guess
but that tells you pretty much
nothing does it about how exactly I feel
when I brush my eyes against the familiar fuzz
of this particular printed letter as it is and therefore
its particular sound somehow and anyway
                        I am writing the words *What Foot*
when I realize that even now when I stand on some
island and stare out at the water and sort of drift

into that space you know water and water and sky
and the drifting and then maybe the thinking I don't need
letters and their looks or syllables and their sounds
and I get way out there on the water in the sky
feeling pretty beautiful actually but then look down
to my foot and the print it inevitably has to make.

What Drama

is it that keeps it from me
what?
      I do wake now
and then to pure beauty
and am, suddenly I am.

      What

could have I been thinking?
Here are two ideas:

1. the cast of characters--
      they're all wrong
  for a drama without
    conflict

2. I am all wrong
  for a drama without
    conflict

      So what

I was wrong. So
    what

I am cycling around
someone pretty without conflict
and find it ok difficult

at first around so much

well

beauty so inoffensive
as to be nearly reflective
of some better part of myself, a self
somehow above conflict yet desirous
of whatever is happening—I mean

could I do without plot as well?
I wake to beauty writ so large
that the usefulness of the basic

elements are called into question.
Beauty is working to erase all the old
dramatic realities: injustices, failures,

and did I say *realities*? I light a candle

because of what for, because

1. it's easy on the eyes

2. everything is *not* an argument
      and every argument
   is not a conflict

       Because ecstasy is illuminated!
        Discovery directed!
      Because I've become the lines!

A candle is invitational they say
candle light makes good stage light

and I am finally believing it
to see it—I mean

now and then when I wake
    to it

What Dignity

At The Meeting I didn't speak
I tried to listen to the tide
above the air conditioner and what
were the people living out of some
outrageously rank suitcases saying?
It seemed important but

I was trying for the waves when
suddenly I was pressed to say
to respond I guess I was frozen
it was unnatural conditioned air
all around me and I wish I hadn't
but I sensed obligation or the like
so I stood and said in a way
wholly my own while their faces
smirked with some sickening self-regard
and something smelling of the one coconut
you definitely do not want to eat

at the meeting I said

oh but I didn't speak

I heard for a while some scheming
but a short while thankfully
some posturing a flapping
a twisting lie a murmur a smirk

then I was only aware of waves fronds that's all

What the Gecko Said

I love the coolness of your windows
invisible and solid and improbable sand
and the world pressed so temptingly beyond
all four of my hands

Also I'm pretty fond of hanging around
upside down: the ceiling one huge blank
page that I never tire of reading
back and forth and back again

I lounge about against your porcelain or
in your tub like a god I survey all
that is mine and yours from the top
of the faucet in light or deepest black

When I call out in lust or otherwise but
mostly lust you hear a tapping as on glass
or a snapping a primal snap or a chortle
as in a quick laugh that spells real ecstasy

There is nothing of yours that I haven't touched
and taken as my own – I scamper I freeze
I tick tick tick from a place you cannot see
life is short I shit where I please I'm hungry

What City

At 86th and 3rd teenagers, a regular gaggle
  of Youth laughed and fought and cried
and kissed and it was around 9 p.m.

on a Friday night and they were painfully
  beautiful though they kept needing
the store front reflections and each other

to tell themselves so. "What's next?"
  they kept asking "What are we doing?"
but they were doing it right there around

86th and 3rd and what's next is something
  they don't really want to know
because it's too much and too soon and what

will one day be reflected will not be
  as nearly beautiful no not nearly as lovely
as all this emotion on a Friday night

the weekend ready to be wasted before them
  given back to them in a store window
one day. I think that I was never a teenager.

Where was I? I wish the question were larger
  somehow. I was in the world of a snow globe
which sits on top of the TV something like eight

thousand miles away in the Pacific, just above
  the equator. The snow globe is of the southern tip
of Manhattan and the Statue of Liberty:

a submerged two-dimensional *brownness* that allows
   the flakes like white boulders to flurry and settle
into a dusting. The TV was on, my side of the world

was turned into its darkest while their side
   flickered and glowed, the Towers flickered
and fell, my eyes flicked to the globe to the TV

to the globe. I lifted it, shook it once.

What Affliction

Hey life is definitely not bad here
lagoon side picture perfect blue sunset
I mean who cares if it's a cliché? Me?

No. Well maybe. I am getting a nice
tan sort of. I stepped on a sea urchin just
last night. I'm really becoming part of the

scene: I've got shells on the window sill here
lagoon side picture perfect blue no green
now sunset boats just floating okay bobbing

right in front of me life is mostly great
sure there is pain and suffering even
next door probably but there's some whiskey

in the cupboard and as I say this view
is not bad with clouds as they are now
floating there above the lagoon above

the boats floating the sun sort of floating
I mean who cares if it's a cliché? Well
ok maybe I do a little bit because I admit

I miss my lovely affliction
which maybe was love or something
to do with love so I'm saying

I'm not telling I'm just going
to sit here and watch the sky
after the sun is very much gone from it

What Answers

Number one it is hot near the sun
and the sun can never say what he wants
and never does what he says.
This causes burning. I forget sometimes
and go to him believing. Also,
it's true the moon is pretty to look at
but talking to her is talking to a rock.
Everyone is happy they got together. Look
how gorgeous and empty they are!

Number two I am water and cannot
help but go everywhere: sometimes
I tire of being pulled and pushed
by the sun and moon because both
are so predictable in their
beauty. You know the rest—

Number three there is all the rest.
Birds, fish, the local trees, coral. All are
unmoved, unfazed, unimpressed. How nice
to be hot and not care, to believe and not
care, to see beauty and not care really.
All the rest is divine, *God* maybe—
tell them this and they laugh and laugh.

Look at me—water! But where do I go?
Some frigates, the fire coral, maybe a coconut,
maybe a mackerel.

What Drifting

I like reading months-old magazines
For the "news" and I like to do this
On an island far away from where
The news happened. A warm climate,

Plenty of time to go fishing and still
Do a good job at work. I like working
Where people still read and maybe even write
Poetry and there is a slow and easy sense

That creation is happening and that it makes
A difference, first for the creator and then
Perhaps others. Is this not risky or "new"?
What else? I like community sports leagues

For the same reason I like my job and I like
Small towns for the same reason I like islands.
None of this requires metaphor though I do
Find it delicious to swim in the very *un*ironic

Attempts we of the Capitol Atoll make to make
Present some experience, handicrafting our way
Through the hours with first one word then
Another then many one over then under the next

And what lovely and delicious purpose we might
Find for it all, maybe, maybe now but ok maybe
Months or years from now and all of it part of
The fantastic story made of distance as in reverie

As in unreal as in the fish that broke free of us.
Because maybe we are sometimes drifting in

The pass and maybe it is someone else's boat we float
Upon and we have our lines down deep deep deep

And the sun is burning down and leaving us
For a while and this too means something—
Because it could mean something and also it simply is.

What Leapt

I sat down with notebook and pen looking
for one of those brilliant sparks as Bill used to
say: then what leapt to mind (in such
a way that reminded me of the pleasure of the image

of *leapt*) were pages from a calendar—numbers
in boxes that were the months to come. I started
filling in the boxes with what quickly became
apparent was what I wanted to come (and was

continuing through the mind) and photocopying and
distributing the plan to certain very essential
individuals (actually everyone was in on the plan—
I visualized copies circulating) but none of this did I

actually record so it began to fade the days erasing
till it was mostly vague what it was then was gone.

But the thing of this thing is that I'd later think
of someone and recognize the essentialness to
some day and so sort of remember a box or two
and what I had wanted to come has been altered some—

this year is a leap year and look I'm putting together
something we've been wanting and look I'm putting
that very something in the extra box so we will
remember and it'll be unspeakably great I can see it here it is:

Three

What Identity

scared of the blank

friends far away thinking of those friends

time on the island has made years
something like eight years yesterday
still ready to step off even further
so far away toward what

is even more blank
the ukulele is tuned to that
occasional rain

I thought the word *sprits* today
there was a rainbow just when I let
a feeling of infidelity enter

tonight I thought of all the faces
that I love while the others *blip*
flickered and *blip* were gone baby

I imagine your face still
scared of the blank too
I'm out here in the blue
thinking thinking of you

all of you eight years twenty
or one and I want to say
there is a child growing in her
that's something

What If

while we play the poet game

it takes me ages to piss.
The girl beside me is impossibly beautiful
but we'll never know exactly something
despite fucking one another very thoroughly.
I mean she is beautiful it can't be
photographed. So beautiful I shouldn't
say. But if the world could
suddenly see her crumbling her flaking—

but it doesn't—it only sees
her stunning lips and the sun
taking a very very long time to come
up. Out of pure loneliness do I wait

before urging it on. I think it best to lie
where you hear the waves.

What Happened

Later, *Homo sapiens* appeared about 60,000 years
ago: evidence in the sediments of the age.
Language emerged. There was need.

After one climate change and before
another, I had depression.
I'll never remember how anything comes
to be or simply ceases.

There was only this pressure on my chest.
These first humans had to adapt
to radically new environments as they
moved south. Some material
was hard to work, you see that don't you?

I've heard that social networks help us
to cope with harsh environmental demands.
Is the urge to flee from others a sign

of a severe climate change? But
I get ahead of myself! Before language
(or After, I can't remember now)
there was the pressure on my chest.
                        But I was watching T.V.

These were modern days after all, and
I was bored, then drawn in... I turned

the channel and there were some animals
that preyed on the misfortunes of others, and some
others obsessed with breeding and this
bit of news seemed somehow very fresh

to me, and just in time.

        *

What Happened Next: Just give me
these simple ontological explanations,
nothing that will make breathing difficult:

abstract ideas like Happiness or, I don't
know, Something Abstract, are too much.

When there is Hunger then Satisfaction
there isn't much to think about.

     Alright, I understand all these thousands
of years are very important, and the ever increasing
complexity of Social Networks can be sort of beautiful
to take in, but making sense
of it wasn't what I needed to be
interested in. I was satisfyingly bored.
Ten thousands years, for example, of progress
and confusion quickly passed, or just passed.

You see what I mean. It was wonderfully
boring! A fabulously anonymous
leaf floating carelessly, effortlessly on the back
of the continual tidal rush of event after event.

What Bikini

Radio Bikini, a film by Robert Stone, begins
with the Japanese surrender,
Truman's atomic bomb "a harness
of the basic power
                              of the universe…"
He thanks God for choosing us to use such power
        for His purposes.

Operation Crossroads
      for the future, our duty

Years later the Iroj of Bikini Atoll recollects the ri-belle general:

"He said he was the most powerful man on earth…
        so many times…why so many times?
    I'd never seen a camera."

An outrigger is gliding there now
   fresh reef fish, a swept yard
     a landing war machine.

Canoes lifted onto navy ships
   in black & white

then The Bomb

not big enough

then another

      and all the navy boys on the sight
   and all the fallout falling out of the sky

    and onto them
    and onto and then into
      the deepest parts of

Bikini
  and onto Rongarik and the islanders there.

      *

Says the American General—
    [take one]
"something good for mankind"
      [take two]
"something good for mankind"
       [take three]
"something good for mankind"
[cut]

"So many times," says the Iroj.

    And "nobody could eat as we were moved away."

      *

Seamen and playing and beer and ice cream
  on the evacuated beaches with station Radio Bikini
      pumping out the hits of 1946.

    "No one told us," say the seamen

  the last personnel out of the lagoon
well protected at 9 miles out…

    "We had nothing to be afraid of."

Delegates from the world
    over
            here to witness: "This
is no threat, no demonstration of WAR."

Able Day and H Hour
the hard-on of the military
journalist as he play-by-plays the take off
from Kwajalein, the "greatest experiment in
human history."   "Bomb's away."

      "…be sure to cover your eyes…"

   "…being from the country…
       it was unbelievable…ahhh look-y there…"

  "…it put me in the mind of the setting sun…"

       "…it was a huge fire cracker…"

"…a keen disappointment from twenty miles away…"

             and then the orders to ground zero

to register the twisted metal
  and the animals they had placed on deck

  and to do some fishing before the next test

      "We didn't know what
          the word was" and the word was

        radioactive—

the Iroj had no idea what it meant,

the General had no idea what it meant.

Then the second test—
    the spray and the fallout—
        the debris.

        "I put a little rock in my pocket."

A doctor says to stay away until it is safe.

Theory into reality, another said.

        *

    Some Bikinian and her beach…
        some coconut
                crackling with reality

What Lagoon

This is another lagoon
like the lagoon I live on
but another; this lagoon
is wilder.
   I do hope
to describe, I cannot hope
to get it. I do not take
pictures. This is wilder:
four shades of blue all
windy and so rolling
toward shore. Here.
Thin white lines as shore.
At least four shades of blue
this Sunday, the other lagoon.
What is distance? I do not
hope. I am not raised to know.
Rolling, white lines, and calm.
Water, sand and green, and water.
I walked yesterday. I rode
some too.
   Continual wind,
I live. This lagoon. Another.
No major statement. Nothing
to report. I put that down.

What Lagoon 2

        I am declaring
this lagoon dead. If there
were coral heads before
they are no longer.
        O mud O splattered
peoples, truly the West and
East have left you
dangerously consuming.
Speeding buses speeding
where? Angry angry young
boys why so far from your-
selves?
        To an outer island!
All of us, quick, away!
        But I am reveling
in this lagoon's beauty. I am
celebrating and trying: brown-blue
water, still water …
        But now, away,
to an outer island, away,
let us away!

What Lagoon 3

Sitting in counsel, the counsel
house home-rest, I listen to these men
talk: another lagoon language moving
(moving?) mingling with the chug
of the generator. Women fry fish.
Mosquitoes feed on us.
        One hour ago three young women
were weaving mats the sun setting
red clouds I thought I was in love
yes I was in love. She wore green
and a smile. What am I doing
here?
        I fluctuate between love
and a vague sort of panic—
tropical depression. I sing
and play my ukulele. There
are children wherever I walk
and they look double look stare
at my browned skin which is
incredibly white.
        Island health island sickness.
Lagoon brown lagoon blue.
        I am not trapped I am not
trapped I am not trapped I am
not trapped I am not.

What Lagoon 4

A night swim
at the causeway
this friendly I-Kiribiti
who when he speaks
English flows like
a native New Zealander's

thoughts of the lovely
girl in green who was
weaving upon my arrival

thoughts of fish

the coolness of
the after-swim

a calming finally
no vague depression

a sort of prayer:
please come funny
play of language, poetry

girl in green maybe
weaving

What Lagoon 5

      A mid-day swoon
and collapse.
      A gift of tobacco to an old
woman. Her story of the three
Gods and this black patch
that no tree stands over—
her gift of tobacco placed
under a giant clam shell
and a prayer. I look down
      to find my left foot
covered in blood.
      A depression where
one thousand Japanese are buried
in her childhood.
      The North Point of Tarawa
where it was made safe
for me to pass to:
empty save for the rotting
missionary complex the missionaries
were forced to abandon just
after building. Signs of offerings.
      My offerings—little fish
and bubble fruit and coconut
and sweet bread. One girl
singing in the counsel house.
      I bathe in the causeway.
      Big breeze nap.

Then the men come back, their nets hanging
      but no fish—
the mosquito starts up,
the generator starts up.

What Lagoon 6

In the lagoon bars little girls
little hottie girls will go go go
if you have a car
little hotties with old local farts
old expat Australians owning the world
this poor world
poor girl
I can almost see your beauty
fading fading before me
such beauty—

where did you learn
the art of disappearing?

The causeway made an island
disappear—now it shows itself
at low tides as a roving bar.

All of South Tarawa is under
piles of garbage. The art
of disappearing—

ripples on still water—

the fading thumps of the minibus
stereo as it screams away.

What Lagoon 7

It's a 2-stroke
It needs a spark plug
Here's a contact too late
Next time another lagoon

The timing is such
I am not so white

I am packing the mask
I am packing the fins
I am taking a nap underwater

It is understood that next time
some clown fish and I will

What I Called Desire

The man I've come to be is made of water
but maybe always was. I am without shape.
Given this state why should this my desire
to fill be a shock; to enter her (or her)
and thereby find, at least for a little spell,
containment, curve of cup, temporary self?

Or to be a deep body, an opened self
that she (or she) may be immersed in water
and allow such disbursement to be a spell
we both are under? Behold! Behold the shape
of it before it's gone forever, when her
eye might fill with a different desire

or something that could stand for desire.
I proclaim this shapeless man to be myself.
I have had to learn not to chase after her
(or her or her) as certainly as water
has to learn not to want to be one shape
only. And so it is I have learned to spell

out who I am each time newly, stay a spell
then trickle on, evaporate desire
without letting vanish the fabulous shape
of wanting, retain the other in the self
for a while for she cannot take in water
that will not soon later be expelled from her.

It is a privilege to be within her
(or her), or have her within me a brief spell
as I've said, before disbursement. This water
runs hot, is beyond what I call desire

and is both myself and now beyond myself
as that thing with potential for any shape

or this thing that can readily give a shape
to being and therefore meaning, which is her
as an empty cup, or her poured into myself,
or her suggestively poised, ready to spell
out who I am now, composed with desire:
The man I've come to be is made of water.

So she gave me shape, so she taught me the spell
we both were under. (Her) and I desired
the other and the self; the cup, the water.

What Was What Is

I used to be this old maple in front of this old house on a narrow
        drive in winter or summer or spring or autumn
But now I am that coconut tree and there are no seasons and the only
        road worth considering is salty and vast

I used to be any number of birds (what a variety of birds!) that come
        and go and build and abandon with the warmth and cold
But now I am this single tern, a speck of white on a blue canvas

I used to be that bird that tree that path
But now I am this bird this tree this path

I used to be an old woman looking out a window
at anything stirring

I used to eat on roof tops with families not my own

Sing this with me: I used to be a planter of seeds
        I used to be a planter of seeds
        But now there are no seasons
        And now I eat alone

I used to know and was sad to know

I used to be hers and hers and hers
But now I am no one's

Sing: I used to have brown eyes
But now I have green, both of them floating

What Fetus

a ball a hoop on the trunk some friends an ocean
straining a pandanus through my teeth
and hey there goes my girl and her sister too
the band's going to practice twice this week
I'm flushing my brain everybody
and my brand new baba just walked up
with fresh donuts in the middle of the night
because my brand new mama wanted
so I have one as well

the palms are rattling their green swords
a gecko clicks from somewhere near
the seawall and it just rained a little
so there is a dripping

it all just flows out of my face
the books are in print on the table
that beater car of mine will run no more
the boat's back in the water
the hole that the super tide made is filled in again
and her stomach is widening

sometimes it's as if there is nothing
between the water's surface and the floor
or what is there drifts through second air

Whatever

It's like hearing *Please Help Me I'm Falling*. An occasional power tool wail.

The ocean and the ocean breeze.
Topics for discussion: I became by accident. My new family

doesn't speak the language.
My days are

a baby not yet born. A timeline
of my life could look like this: Born. Kissed a girl. Missed something

important. Kissed another then another girl. Decided on the loveliest
who decided on me. So on it goes. I remember the day at the beach.

There will be a child.
I am from a place I now have no memory of.

The swimming is fine.

The place is special exactly because its history is being erased.
I feel as though I've never completed a thought.
Over time, what? All jobs are traditional.

So far
I've learned that minds open and close. I became and it was

an accident.
I became because I wanted

to learn: the islands
were green with Love. The girl who kissed me and grew

with child. Her work is the most difficult of all and so I bow my
head.

P. K. Harmon is the former theatre director and Humanities professor of the College of the Marshall Islands from 2001 to 2005 and was a Visiting Poet and Professor of Creative Writing for the University of Pittsburgh at Johnstown from 2006 to 2009.

Over the past twenty-five years, Harmon has lived and worked in a variety of cultures outside his native Appalachia: Guyana in South America; Istanbul, Turkey; Amsterdam, Holland; the Marshall Islands in eastern Micronesia; Guam; and Hawai'i. He has worked in the theatre during this time, both as a director and an actor, most recently in starring roles for main stage productions for the University of Guam's Fine Arts Theatre. He is a songwriter, too, recently for the band Bikini Test Go Ahead, a do-it-yourself punk-folk affair whose offerings are apocalyptic love songs centered on the nuclear heritage of the Marshall Islands. Free downloads are available at the artists' collective web page www.myideaoffun.org.

Born in Louisville, Kentucky in 1968, P. K. Harmon is a graduate of the Creative Writing Program at Ohio University in Athens, Ohio. In 2004, he edited an anthology of poetry by Marshall Islanders entitled *Al En Aleon Kine*, published by Micronitor Press. He is the winner of the 2011-2012 Serving House Fairleigh-Dickinson First Book Prize in Poetry for his collection *What Island*. In 2012, he was featured in YARN's National Poetry Project "Crossing Country Line by Line". From 2010 until 2014, he held various editorial positions for *Storyboard: A Journal of Pacific Imagery*, published at the University of Guam. He has had poems published recently in *Riverwind*, *The Marshall Islands Journal*, the *Micronesian Educator*, *Blackmail Press*, the *Southeast Review*, and *Gesture Literary Review*.

At present, he and his two children, both native Marshall Islanders born on Majuro, live in Mangilao on the island of Guam.

Cover Artist

Mark Hackworth is an artist living in Athens, Ohio. He has exhibited his work nationally and internationally. Permanent collections include: Cleveland Museum of Art (book collection), Denison University, Hudson River Editions (New York). He has designed book covers for *Riverwind Literary Magazine* and *The Pikeville Review*. He is the director of the art program at Hocking College where he teaches photography and drawing.

Acknowledgements

Grateful acknowledgement is made to the editors of publications in which these poems, or versions of them, first appeared:

The Laurel Review: "What Was What Is," "What City"
The Marshall Islands Journal: "What Drifting"
Riverwind: "What Wave," "What Moon," "What Shape," "What I Say," "What Lips

Many thanks to the following good people, without whom this collection could not have been realized:

Joe Murphy, in the Marshall Islands; J. A. Nash, in Australia; Mark Hackworth, Jacob Koestler, Wendy McVicker, Pat Brown, Jill Rosser, and Rosemarie Basile, in Athens, Ohio; Deni Naffziger, Jane Ann Devol Fuller, Bonnie Proudfoot, and Jeffery Hanson of Hocking College; Kathy Kloss and Fred Fornoff of the University of Pittsburgh at Johnstown; Paula Odile Wessels, in Holland; Arzu Unal, in Istanbul, Turkey; C. S. Schreiner of the University of Guam; Sarah Strickley; Derek Archer of the University of Guyana; Patrice Mutchnick; and Sarah Johnson and Chris Knights, who know a little something of the beaches of this world.

Thanks to Wayne Dodd, Tom Andrews, Kristi Leatherwood, Josie Bloomfield, and Mark Halliday—great teachers all.

For helping me to make a handful of these poems into songs for the band Bikini Test Go Ahead, thank you Dan Oatman, a singular talent. Thanks to the band: Dallas Zimmerman, Sean Jackson, Mike Miller, and Matt Miller. Thanks to Mike McDermit, Laci Hess, Laura McAllister, Brandon Locher, and the entire MyIdeaOfFun artist collective—here is number 210.

Bethany Goch was an empathetic and careful reader of these poems as they struggled into some sort of completion. Her insights came at a crucial time.

Special thanks to Claire Bateman and Mark Halliday for spending time with the book in its final stages.

Eric Schwerer is a great friend and a great poet. From even when they were little surf-smooth thoughts in my head, he saw every poem through to the page. Thank you, Eric, for everything.

And thank you, David E. and Paula Harmon, for building a library. Here is one slim addition.

www.ingramcontent.com/pod-product-compliance
Lightning Source LLC
Chambersburg PA
CBHW031208090426
42736CB00009B/833